Let's EXPLORE

baby einstein®

Colors

The WALT DISNEY Company

Fine Art Credits:
The publisher would like to thank the following museums for their kind permission to reprint these paintings by Vincent van Gogh: *Lane in the Public Garden at Arles*, from the collection of the Kroller-Muller Museum, Otterlo, The Netherlands • *Fourteen Sunflowers in a Vase*, by permission of The National Gallery, London, photograph © The National Gallery, London • *The Starry Night*, by permission of The Museum of Modern Art, New York, Acquired through the Lillie P. Bliss Bequest, photograph © The Museum of Modern Art, New York • *Orchard in Blossom with View of Arles, Fishing Boats on the Beach at Saintes-Maries-de-la-Mer*, and *Wheat Fields with Reaper at Sunrise*, by permission of the Van Gogh Museum (Vincent van Gogh Foundation), Amsterdam.

Hyperion Books for Children, New York
For information address Hyperion Books for Children, 114 Fifth Avenue, New York, New York 10011-5690.
Printed in China
Library of Congress Cataloging Card Number on file.
ISBN 0-7868-3803-5

Visit www.hyperionbooksforchildren.com and www.babyeinstein.com

Great Minds Start Little.™

red

Where can you see the
color red in this painting?

Can you find all the sailboats?

Fishing Boats on the Beach at Saintes-Maries-de-la-Mer

"It is the painting that makes me so happy these days."
—Vincent van Gogh

orange

Why do you think these flowers
are called sunflowers?

Do you ever see flowers outside?
Do they look like this?

Fourteen Sunflowers in a Vase

*"Painting as it is now promises to become more subtle—
more like music and less like sculpture—and above all
it promises color. If only it keeps this promise."*
—Vincent van Gogh

yellow

Can you find the things that are yellow?

Look closely and try to find three little houses.

Wheat Fields with Reaper at Sunrise

"There is a sun, a light that for want of another word I can only call yellow, pale sulphur yellow, pale golden citron. How lovely yellow is!"
—Vincent van Gogh

green

Which shade of green is lightest in this painting? Which is darkest?

What time of year do you think it is in this painting — winter, spring, summer, or fall? Why?

Lane in the Public Garden at Arles

"I am always in hope of making a discovery by a wedding of two complementary colors, their mingling and opposition, the mysterious vibration of kindred spirits."
—Vincent van Gogh

blue

The sky is blue in this painting.
Is there a blue sky outside
your window?

Can you find the moon
in this painting?

The Starry Night

*"I often think the night is more alive and
more richly colored than the day."*
—Vincent van Gogh

purple

Where did the artist use purple?
What other colors can you see?

Are any of your toys purple?

Orchard in Blossom with View of Arles

"As long as autumn lasts, I shall not have hands, canvas and
colors enough to paint the beautiful things I see."
—Vincent van Gogh

Which bike is red?

Can you point to the yellow fruit?

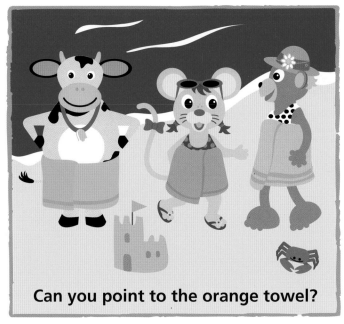

Can you point to the orange towel?

Can you point to the green lollipop?

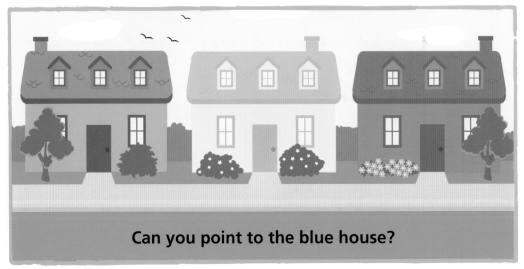

Can you point to the blue house?

Which clown is wearing the purple hat?